GREENHOUSE GARDENING FOR BEGINNERS

Your Ultimate and Complete Guide to Learn How to Create a DIY Container Gardening and Grow Vegetables at Home and How to Manage a Miniature Indoor Greenhouse.

© Copyright 2021 by Viktor Garden - All rights reserved.

The following Book is reproduced below with the goal of providing information that is as accurate and reliable as possible. Regardless, purchasing this Book can be seen as consent to the fact that both the publisher and the author of this book are in no way experts on the topics discussed within and that any recommendations or suggestions that are made herein are for entertainment purposes only. Professionals should be consulted as needed prior to undertaking any of the action endorsed herein.

This declaration is deemed fair and valid by both the American Bar Association and the Committee of Publishers Association and is legally binding throughout the United States.

Furthermore, the transmission, duplication, or reproduction of any of the following work including specific information will be considered an illegal act irrespective of if it is done electronically or in print. This extends to creating a secondary or tertiary copy of the work or a recorded copy and is only allowed with the express written consent from the Publisher. All additional right reserved.

The information in the following pages is broadly considered a truthful and accurate account of facts and as such, any inattention, use, or misuse of the information in question by the reader will render any resulting actions solely under their purview. There are no scenarios in which the publisher or the original author of this work can be in any fashion deemed liable for any hardship or damages that may befall them after undertaking information described herein.

Additionally, the information in the following pages is intended only for informational purposes and should thus be thought of as universal. As befitting its nature, it is presented without assurance regarding its prolonged validity or interim quality. Trademarks that are mentioned are done without written consent and can in no way be considered an endorsement from the trademark holder.

Table of Contents

GREENHOUSE GARDENING FOR BEGINNERS 1
- INTRODUCTION 8
- CHAPTER 1: TYPES OF GREENHOUSE 13
  - *Other types of structures* 15
  - *Screen houses* 15
  - *Crop upper structures* 16
  - *Classifying Greenhouse* 16
  - *Low Technology Greenhouses* 17
  - *Medium-technology greenhouses* 18
  - *High-technology greenhouses* 19
- CHAPTER 2: CONSTRUCTING A GREENHOUSE 20
  - *Orientation* 22
  - *Length-width ratio* 23
  - *A good rule of thumb can be a 3: 1 size ratio.* 24
  - *Foundations* 24
  - *Roof Slope* 25
  - *Insulation* 28
  - *Beds and Paths* 28
- CHAPTER 3: PLANNING FOR A GREENHOUSE 31
  - *Budget Plans* 81
  - *Material options* 83
- CHAPTER 4: GREENHOUSE ENVIRONMENT 87
  - *Greenhouse Lighting Control* 89
  - *Humidity control* 90
- CHAPTER 5: ESSENTIAL GREENHOUSE EQUIPMENT 96
  - *Lighting* 101
  - *Digital Thermometer* 101
- CHAPTER 6: USING SPACE EFFECTIVELY 103
- CHAPTER 7: GROWING IN YOUR GREENHOUSE 109
- CHAPTER 8: SCHEDULING PLANTS OF YEAR-ROUND GROWING 119
- CHAPTER 9: HYDROPONICS IN A GREENHOUSE 129
- CHAPTER 10: PESTS AND DISEASES 139
- CHAPTER 11: TEMPERATURE AND LIGHT REQUIREMENTS OF YOUR PLANT .. 151
  - *Directional Exposure:* 154
- CONCLUSION 159

Introduction

A greenhouse (also called a glasshouse, or, if with adequate heating, a hothouse) can be a structure with walls and ceilings, mainly transparent materials such as glass, during which plants in need of a regulated climate Are grown. These structures range in size from small sheds to industrial-sized buildings. A miniature greenhouse is understood as a chili frame. The greenhouse exposed to sunlight becomes significantly warmer than the outside temperature, protecting its contents in the weather.

Many commercial glass greenhouses or hothouses are high-tech production facilities for vegetables, flowers, or fruits. Glass greenhouses are littered with equipment, including screening installations, heating, cooling, lighting, and controlled by a computer to optimize conditions for plant growth. Different techniques are then used to evaluate the optimum temperature degree and luxury ratio of a greenhouse, such as air temperature, balance, and vapor-pressure losses, to measure production risk before cultivating the selected crop.

<u>Greenhouses leave more control over plant growing environments. The significant factors that can be controlled include temperature, sunlight and shade levels, irrigation, fertilizer use, and atmospheric humidity, depending on the greenhouse's technical specification. Conservatories may also be accustomed to overcoming deficiencies within a small amount of ground growing properties, such as brief weather or low light level, and that they can improve food production in marginal environments. Shade houses are used to supply shade, especially in hot, dry climates.</u>

<u>Since those few crops can be grown throughout the year, greenhouses are essential in the food supply of high-latitude countries. One of the most critical complexes within the world is Almería, Andalusia, Spain, where greenhouses cover about 200 km2 (49,000 acres).</u>

Greenhouses are often used for flowers, vegetables, fruits, and transplants. Particular greenhouse types of some crops, like tomatoes, are typically used for commercial production.

Many vegetables and flowers are often grown in greenhouses in late winter and early spring, then transplanted due to the weather outside. Seed tray racks may also be used to stack seed trays inside the greenhouse for later planting outside. Hydroponics (especially hydroponic A-frames) are often used to make the most important indoor space use while growing crops in mature shapes inside greenhouses.

Bumblebees are often used as pollinators for pollination, but other types of bees have also been used, even as artificial pollination.

The relatively closed environment of the greenhouse has its unique management requirements when compared to outdoor production. Pests and diseases, extremes of temperature and humidity, need to be controlled, and irrigation is essential for water supply. Most greenhouses use sprinklers or drip lines. Especially with the winter production of hot-season vegetables, significant heat and light inputs may also be required.

Greenhouses also have applications outside the agricultural industry. Glass point Solar, located in Fremont, California, engages solar fields in greenhouses to supply steam for solar-augmented oil recovery. For example, in November 2017, Glass point announced developing a solar augmented oil recovery facility near Bakersfield, CA, that uses greenhouses to surround its parabolic troughs.

An "alpine house" can be a unique greenhouse that is used to grow alpine plants. The purpose of an alpine house is to mimic the conditions during which alpine plants grow; Especially in winter, to protect from wet conditions. Alpine homes are often not heated, as the plants grew there are hardy or require the most protection from harsh frost within the winter. They possess excellent ventilation.

CHAPTER 1: TYPES OF GREENHOUSE

Greenhouse classification corresponds to its original size. Types include gable, flat arch, raised dome, sawtooth, tunnel.

Multi-span structures

Multi-span greenhouses have a smaller area than single-span greenhouses with similar production capacity in different regions. This leads to less heat loss and significant energy savings. Significant economies of scale and production capacity are also attainable using multi-span design.

Multi-spans are generally more robust in design. As a result, they tend to suffer less damage during hurricanes and thunderstorms winds.

Other types of structures

Shed houses

Shed houses are covered in woven or otherwise manufactured materials to allow sunlight, moisture, and air to pass through the gap. Building materials are employed to supply a specific environmental modification, such as protection from low light or severe weather. The crest of the structure will suit different types of crops and should be equal to 8 meters.

Shed houses are used on outdoor hydroponic systems, especially in hot areas.

Screen houses

Screen houses are structures that are covered in insect screening materials rather than plastic or glass. They supply environmental modification and protection from severe weather as an exclusion of pests. They often seek to obtain many benefits of greenhouses in hot or tropical climates.

Crop upper structures

A crop top may be a structure with a roof, but which does not have walls. Roof covering can also be greenhouse construction materials such as plastic or glass, shade cloth, or insect screening. These structures provide some modification of the growing environment, such as crop protection from rain or reduction in sunshine levels.

Classifying Greenhouse

The greenhouse is a technology-based investment. The higher the technology used, the greater the ability to achieve tightly controlled growing conditions. It is the ability to tightly control the conditions during which the crop is grown, strongly associated with crop health and productivity. The latter three categories of greenhouses are defined to help people select the appropriate investment for their needs and budget.

Low Technology Greenhouses

A significant proportion of the industry in Australia currently uses low technology structures. These greenhouses are 3 meters in total height. Tunnel houses, or "igloos," are the most common type. They do not have vertical walls. They need poor ventilation. Such a structure is comparatively inexpensive and straightforward. Little or no automation is employed.

While this type of structure provides a primary advantage over field production, crop capacity is limited by the growing environment, and crop management is comparatively difficult. Low-level greenhouses usually end up in an ever-increasing subtropical climate that restricts yields and does little to reduce pests and diseases. Pest and disease control, as a result, is usually structured around a chemical spray program.

Low-technology greenhouses have significant production and environmental limitations, but they provide a price-effective entry for the industry.

Medium-technology greenhouses

Medium-level greenhouses typically feature vertical walls 2 m but 4 m tall and a full-height 5.5 m. They will be roof or sidewall ventilation or both. Medium-level greenhouses generally are attached to single or double skin film or glass and use varying automation degrees.

Medium-level greenhouses form a compromise between cost and productivity and represent a reasonable economic and environmental basis for the industry. Production in medium-level greenhouses is often more efficient than field production. Hydroponic systems increase the efficiency of water use. There is a huge opportunity to use non-chemical pest and disease management strategies, but it is difficult to achieve the full potential of greenhouse gardening overall.

High-technology greenhouses

High-level greenhouses have a minimum wall height of 4 meters, with the top-level eight meters above ground level. These structures provide better crop and environmental performance. Technology structures will have roof ventilation and even have sidewall vents.

Cladding can also be film (single or double), polycarbonate sheeting, or glass. Environmental controls are almost always automated.
These structures provide enormous opportunities for economic and ecological sustainability. Pesticide use is often significantly reduced. Technology structures typically provide impressive vision and are increasingly becoming involved in agribusiness opportunities internationally.

Although these are greenhouse capital intensive, they provide a highly productive, environmentally sustainable opportunity for a complex, fresh produce industry. Wherever possible, investment decisions, technology should be kept in the greenhouse.

CHAPTER 2: CONSTRUCTING A GREENHOUSE

Greenhouse freestanding greenhouse is often an excellent opportunity to build an entirely new location with few restrictions. My Phoenix Greenhouse at CRMPI is a perfect example of using design flexibility, picking and choosing details from below, while offering as much potential as possible for high-end performance.

However, the prices inherent in building a heavily insulated northern wall are often significant. For this reason, it does not make much sense to create a slightly freestanding greenhouse; They tend to form and become inefficient until they are of sufficient size. I like to recommend minimum dimensions of 12 × 30 feet. Without an enclosed structure, this backup is more likely to desire heat, counting on the step of the climatic zone you want to feel.

Enclosed greenhouses provide an oasis away from your home, reducing construction costs through the winter due to additional lebensraum, shared heating, and a preexisting north wall. They will be of any size, and they do not require different paths and infrastructure that would be a separate structure. An enclosed greenhouse at an equivalent time almost certainly impedes surface viewing and can introduce insects into your home without a screen. They pose some risk of unwanted humidity without sliding glass doors and proper ventilation. Also, your designs are bound to be tied to the house's odd conditions that you just want to take back.

Orientation

The optimal orientation for a greenhouse in North America is generally directed to the south or southeast. In cold climates, it is essential to capture the morning sun for the first time. The east-facing orientation may also work, especially if there is some glazing along with the southern display. In most situations, western orientation or exposure to overheating ability should be avoided.

By the way, these recommendations should be considered guidelines and not hard and fast rules; It is essential to oversee your situation. In areas where it is very cloudy for the winter, as in the northwest, the orientation is a small amount because clouds spread sunshine throughout the sky. Also, at high latitudes, the summer sun moves much further north.

Length-width ratio

A less wide greenhouse does not have a window for a solar gain during the day. At CRMPI, I think the greenhouse is 24 × 35 feet and does not work either because of Phoenix's 76 × 26-foot dimensions. This difference is because the sun remains too much to heat an area along the extended east-western axis within the daytime. This is a significant consideration if you are building a freestanding greenhouse.

A good rule of thumb can be a 3:1 size ratio.

Foundations

There are many different materials and methods for building foundations, and you will use any to put other structures together in a greenhouse. The most recent foundations I have used at CRMPI are the structure's framing and concrete piers. The first two greenhouses used pressurized treated wood posts for the foundation plants.

It is easy to overline the Greenhouse Foundation because they only catch glazing and the occasional snow load. Still, your approach to calculating and allowing engineering regulations in your area, your options may also be limited. Liability concerns may also be an element during school or professional settings.

Roof Slope

Although Phoenix's roof features a 4/12 slope (falling 4 inches for each leg of length), in ecosystem design, we typically shed heavy snow loads for the 6/12 pitch, which is the climate of the region—based on. Because the greenhouse is warmer than surface air, a layer of snowflakes is often formed between polycarbonate glazing and ice, which helps the roof shed any ice of serious weight. Snowfall tends to reside in doubly increased poly.

Relative to the roof's slope is the freeboard, the space between the lower floor of the top and, therefore, the ground. In areas with heavy snowfall, a minimum of 3 or 4 feet is sweetened so that the greenhouse roof does not cause snow piles or obstruction.

Framing and glazing materials are two common framing materials, wood, and metal. Wood is excellent for small greenhouses and has the advantage of being an inexpensive, familiar material that is easy to install with or without special equipment. Salved, rough-sawn, or beetle-kill lumber are available quickly. Wood requires more maintenance; Although relying on wood, it can easily last fifty years during a dry climate with the right color and care.

Today almost all commercial greenhouses are constructed with galvanized steel, often added over a long chain. Kit greenhouses are most often made of steel, and so the fasteners and directions involved can make assembly much more effortless. Galvanized steel has a longer shelf life than wood and does not require staining, sealing, or much maintenance. As shown by Phoenix's roof slope, steel framing often provides less flexibility in construction, mostly when shielded from other projects.

Glazing options are continually evolving. The six-mm double-inflated poly is cheaper, more flexible, and less insulating, while expensive, rigid polycarbonate panels last longer and have better delays against ice. Double-flowered poly was a great inexpensive option within the early years at CRMPI, and it works well on the roof of many of our greenhouses.

Glass is often suitable for eastern or southern walls but should only be used for vertical glazing due to weight. Expansion and contraction can cause mounting problems, and glass presents a more significant problem than polycarbonate or plastic when broken. It is generally more expensive and less insulating than polycarbonate and can also pronounce direct sunlight, which can also burn plants in some cases.

Insulation

Insulation is essential on the north wall and therefore on the west wall; Confirm insulating all walls you are not glazing on. Foam insulation or structural insulated panels (SIPs) work well but must be sealed and dried - they are not rated for moisture in the greenhouse. I used these panels when building Phoenix, but commercially, we started using metal siding against Styrofoam directly within the SIP to eliminate any wood products. There is plenty of room to apply your preferred method here. Straw bales are a well-liked natural building method but are not an honest consideration used during greenhouses due to the potential for mold problems in high-moisture environments.

Beds and Paths

People often want to keep in extensive paths to accommodate carts and wheels but think twice about using your greenhouse.

After the bed's initial construction and preparation, there is not much to bring the fabric in and out in large quantities. Here at CRMPI, I make small paths to maximize the growth path, and I place an outdoor area near the door to bring mulch and material with fifteen-gallon nursery pots.

Microclimates microclimate created
Each greenhouse replacement inside it, but within which the microclimate will propagate. These are being produced by your design and therefore must change with the material used and thermal mass over time by water tanks, more plant biomass, or new infrastructure.

While the greenhouse climate will be mostly homogenous, it is vital to cultivate a rich microclimate to help establish thriving plants.

For example, cold air sinks, so if your greenhouse has two levels or slopes, the pathways under the rock will be a chilly sink, so the outer edges of the space will be cold within the winter, where they lose heat. Surface. By installing circulating fans, you will help reduce this problem. The southwest corner will usually be the greenest and hottest quadrant of the greenhouse because it is exposed to the sun at the forefront. The Northeast is cooling and maybe the right place for a dissemination table or washing station. Remember how plant growth will create shady areas over time, and plan for their tallest perennials within the northwest, often the tallest point of the greenhouse.

CHAPTER 3: PLANNING FOR A GREENHOUSE

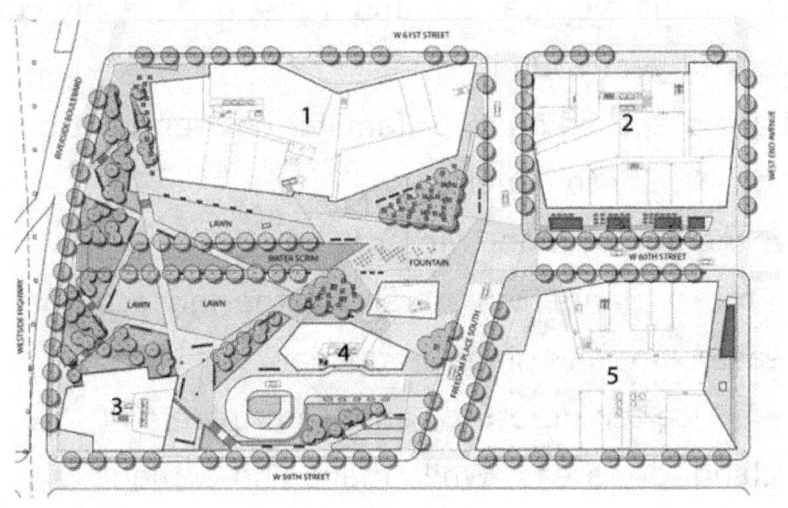

Its origins as a luxury habit for a great man and therefore privileged, greenhouses are now used in important and eye-opening ways that humans understand and use nature naturally. It has been finding its way into commercial use since World War II, feeding the world's population. Individually, a greenhouse can benefit you in many ways: access to

Fresh greens, vegetables, and fruits, and freshly cut flowers all year round
that are prepared for your familiar environment or season. Ability to develop.
Traveling during a hot winter wind
can protect plants from harsh weather, insects that increase plant and plant production
help reduce temperatures and water plants in scorching, dry areas. While managing damage
adds beauty and visual appeal to your landscape

, so, you are considering one. Greenhouse. This is a serious investment that must be planned over time. With ideas that need attention, it is difficult to understand where to begin. But today, we will take things a lot less by giving necessary guidelines, meeting the necessary guidelines, meeting the requirements, incorporating the budget tips, and choosing the right location according to the meteorological considerations. Whether you are a beginner or an experienced professional, you will get new ideas from this guide for thinking to build a greenhouse in your home garden.

The right location can only be a possible place to plant a greenhouse in your garden. But if you are making a choice, then it is worth giving you the best possible location. With careful site selection, you will optimize your greenhouse structure's productivity, which helps you offset the space that your garden will take, which is also your initial outlay, considering the time and energy spent in construction. Increases

You will need a location that has the highest risk for radiation.

Your plants require a minimum of six hours of exposure to sunlight for photosynthesis. This method is essential for the plants to be healthy and to grow fruits or flowers. The most straightforward seating direction depends mostly on the season on which you want to plant.

East-West Facing Ridge. Lining the structure's ridge to maximize light interception from east to west, especially during November to January. The direction will help warm the crops more quickly after the cold nights.

South Facing Ridge. By the time you plan to grow your crop during the summer, this sitting position is better. The direction will distribute equal amounts of sunlight to each side of the structure, and excessive heat reduces the temperature.

Further note: If possible, avoid the edge of a part of your home because the amount of sunlight in this area is limited by the plants until you are ready to facilitate additional sources of sunlight and heat. Also, consider that the shady area will limit the amount of sun your greenhouse receives. Shed lines vary between summer and winter. It is advised that the greenhouse should be at least twice sufficient distance from any potential shade source's crest.

Recent research also suggests that a site's latitude should be a basis for your preferred orientation on your structure. For example, for southern latitudes where there is a warmer temperature, a north-south orientation is perfect for supplying good light and the best ventilation. Also, wind strength and direction should be considered. Outdoor gardening is challenging in winding areas. Choose a place where you have windproofing like trees but confirm that this does not cause excessive flashing.

Ensure that there is easy access to water, electricity, and other essential utilities at the location. You will need a place with almost water use, heat, and electricity for convenient gardening. The water system is critical, especially in horticulture, that a natural source of water such as rain or groundwater is restricted. In laying one, it is best to review your land profile. Better yet, choose a place where you will successfully irrigate your water. It also serves as the equivalent of the power required to provide electricity with lawnmowers, hedge trimmers, outdoor lights, pond pumps, and greenhouse heaters. Care should be taken to avoid fire and lightning.

A stable elevation ground is essential to prevent unnecessary water accumulation. While watering is critical for plant expansion, they will also suffer or die from overgrowth caused by rain flooding or excess water coming from the roof. It is best to build your structure for high ground, so the runoff flows far from the small greenhouse.

Note further: It is technically possible to orient a greenhouse on a slope but avoid doing so. You will need a better elevation ground, but planting it during the slope's base will make the pockets cool, where the coolness is mainly for winter farming.

Find a site that has honest soil to grow plants or has the potential to become. If you are almost sure of the soil's outline, you will need to hire an expert to research the nutrient, texture, and composition of your soil. Digging into organic material often leads to soil improvement. But unless you are ready to find a neighborhood that has excellent horticultural soil and natural drainage, less preparation is required when plowing into it, reducing weed seed banks, and adding organic matter Is included.

Further Note: Attempt to avoid stony or rocky ground as hiccups often occur within the construction process.

Finally, the ability to expand a space is additionally useful. The need for expansion is usually unpredictable. You will need a larger space for your growing crops; otherwise, the number of your plants may increase. It is always ideal for building a greenhouse over a large area to meet the possibility of expansion.

Allocate space

How much space do you need? As mentioned, your chosen location should provide enough room for you to expand for years to return. Additionally, the allocated space should justify the borrowed space in your garden. In many instances, greenhouse owners either find themselves rarely needing additional space or needing square footage. To avoid these common mistakes, it is necessary to measure the factors that usually occur during the greenhouse.

The plants you want to sue. Initially, compact space for seed planting is employed. As plants grow, you must triple the length. A 10 'x 10' is usually the minimum size for potted plants. But cabin-friendly greenhouses require less space. Even a 6 'x 6' is already a cure. For better farming, where planters grow plants on the ground, walking requires that they walk well enough to walk. When production time comes, you will have to work by harvesting the plant first in the center area.

Isles, walkways, and dealing space. It is a standard practice to move away from enough walking space to see and harvest the plants. Generally, 40 percent of the ground area is for corridors and walkways. With a minimum 18-inch work corridor in the middle and a one to the three-to-five-foot main hall in the middle, you will potentially increase the mounting space by a minimum of 10 percent. This method also provides quick access to moving plants with a cart.

Bonus tip: a one-meter overall structure of space is essential not only for easy access to the greenhouse but is also useful in cases where maintenance issues arise. For example, exchanging pan or cover or cleaning would be easier if you were allocated enough space to walk past. Leaving this space would also mean that fences and other structures are not sufficient to tie ventilation or close unwanted shadows. Leaving generous space at the front is additionally wise as the opening door is separate for ventilation and air circulation.

Benches, Racks, Hanging Baskets. These are all extras but can also make up the most important of space. The courts usually want to use the space for the assembly area. It works well for crops like ground cover. Traditionally 60–90 percent length benches typically contribute to the ground area. Configuration wise, floating trays are more efficient. Others prefer hanging baskets to increase space utilization. Hanging basket conveyors are attached to overhead trusses where the plants are spaced eight inches apart. For plants with large rooms, an A-frame rack system can double your growing space. They will be constructed with 2 'x 4' wood and fence pipes or heavy steel rods. However, if you only need a few to plant your plants from the bottom, the shelves will be in a pinch and box for small spaces.

Irrigation and Drainage. These two factors can eat up space. Drip irrigation will not be a drag for vast and large greenhouses, except in a small setup, one can be prepared to use water efficiently by hand. Meanwhile, floor drainage should begin with a gravel or stone base six to eight inches below the ground.

like plants

If you are new to gardening, it is best to know which plants will be best in your greenhouse. It can also rely heavily on your setup due to your greenhouse's ability to regulate environmental factors. However, plants suitable for greenhouse gardening are available for every cool greenhouse and climate. They are grouped into three categories: Vegetables and crops, fruits, and ornaments.

Vegetables and Crop

For beginners, it is sensible to start with easy vegetables that will give you an edge over the basic principles of growth within a year. You will continue with complex crops as you raise your hands on them. Here are some samples of plants that snowball in your greenhouse.

Leafy Shak Bhaji. Veggies that belong to lettuce, like lettuce, grow in the same way, especially when considering bed plants.

Black pepper. Nearly every type of chili can grow well during a greenhouse. They are best placed during temperatures of 15 inches apart and above 55 degrees Fahrenheit.

Tomatoes: With sufficient sunlight and a steady night temperature of at least 55 degrees Fahrenheit, tomatoes can grow exceptionally well in a greenhouse.

Microbe. Rich in the nutritious punch, microgreens are ideal for family-oriented greenhouses. These are small tender versions of familiar vegetables. There is a desire to diversify producers by taking varieties such as Boricuas, Arugula, or Spicy-type-greens. They sprout them and allow these small crops to grow every week or two.

Herb. Most of the seed-growing plants are probably the simplest to grow. They need a little attention. If you have simple control over your greenhouse temperature, you will not face any problems growing them. Common popular herbs in the greenhouse include basil, cilantro, tarragon, rosemary, and thyme and

Other hot weather vegetables. These summer crops require a high intensity of a minimum of 60 ° F during daytime and a minimum of 55 ° F in the dark. Many types of vegetables within this classification were best during a greenhouse. These include beans, cucumbers, brinjals, cantaloupe, and summer squash.

Other Winter Vegetables. It is best to grow winter vegetables in a greenhouse because they fail to pollinate in hot temperatures. These crops require a daytime temperature of 50–70 ° F and 45–55 ° F in the dark. This cold season's vegetables include beets, cabbage, cauliflower, broccoli, carrots, charas, turnips, peas, and radishes.

Fruit

Growing fruits demand a warm climate. Most fruit trees appreciate temperatures above 50 degrees Fahrenheit whereas above 60 Fahrenheit for tropical fruits. But even in unheated greenhouses, a wide variety of fruits can be raised in a surprisingly carefree manner.

Citrus fruits. You will increase the spread of oranges, lemons, and tangerines in the greenhouse. They require strength to maintain the coldest weather. They only need temperatures around 55 degrees Fahrenheit to germinate and survive in winter.

Peaches and Nectarines. Newbies generally prefer peaches because they are nutritious and straight to handle. Along with nectar, both are often grown in hot or cold greenhouses.

Grapes. Growing vines always involve high temperatures. With proper ventilation and heating, the greenhouse is often an ideal place to grow grapes. Certain types of grapes can also thrive under cold climates, such as Black Hamburg and Buckland Sweetwater.

Further note: Grapevine requires tons of room. A vine owes a lot to a little greenhouse. One meter should be allocated between each vine. If getting aggressive for your garden space is essential to gauge.

Organelles are in demand and can be a legitimate source of income. It beautifies a landscape and can also be a decorative addition to any home. Whatever the reason for your growth, you will find different types of jewelry that will excel in any cool greenhouse.

Flower bearing plants. One of the advantages of obtaining a greenhouse is the possibility of supplying blooming plants throughout the year. With appropriate lighting and solar heating, you will be ready to grow many exciting and colorful flowers.

Flax or Shade-Loving Annual: These beautiful ornaments hold beautiful pendant flowers that make them ideal for hanging baskets. Petal-filled blooms appear in many colors, and some selections have variegated leaves. In each season, gardeners start with some or more types of **shade flowers.** Favorites are Elysium, Begonia, Ladies Airdrop, Impotence, Hypo Estes, and Angel Wing Caladium.

Perennials: These stem flowers are your best source of freshly cut flowers. Compared to annual plants, perennials can grow up to 2 seasons and thrive exceptionally when grown during a greenhouse due to its ideal controlled temperature. The plants are usually developed during a greenhouse during winter and brought from outside to fill the garden in summer. The favorite arrays that make up a perennial garden are anemones, tulip bulbs, lilies, esters, chrysanthemum, decks, gaillardias, rosés, and hyacinths.

Bushes and Mountaineers. A number of these varieties cannot be grown successfully in an open garden and wish to conserve a greenhouse. Dedicated climbers take up little ground space and are excellent choices for small greenhouses, while wall bushes require more ground space. Popular plants are Clematis, Shrub Rose, Wisteria, and Honeysuckle.

Tropical. Even tropical plants require warm temperatures that can be an area during a greenhouse. Suppose you want to grow something more diverse. In that case, greenhouses are often an ideal setting for tropical plants such as cacti, orchids, Venus flytrap, and other carnivorous plants if you only pay attention to indoor conditions.

Greenhouse

The type you prefer depends on where you live and what you want to grow. From functionality to aesthetics, greenhouses are also being designed to suit design and elegance. The following are inspiring greenhouses that you want to think about classified supported environmental temperature requirements, functionality, appearance, and construction.

Cold house temperature (temperature: below freezing). The strategy is to start the fall of crops early and extend the season in the spring. This still protects plants despite not having an additional heat source.

Cool house (temperature: 45-50F). Planning is conducted by creating an area ready to capture maximum light and maximum amount of heat from the sun. Already heat is redistributed during darkness, which plants may not adapt to extreme cold.

Warm houses (temperature: 55F). These greenhouses are specifically designed to work during the coldest times of the year when sunlight is at its minimum. It protects plants from adverse weather through a transparent roof enclosure that is generally built to the bottom. The first task is to allow a wide range of plants to survive.

Warm houses (temperature: 60F). Install such supplemental heat. Friendly homes often want to grow tropical plants.

According to design or structure

A plethora of styles are available to organize but are the most common types used later.

A-frame. A decorated ceiling and side walls are the significant features of the design. The main advantage is that minimal use of materials is sufficient to satisfy the desire for greenhouse production.

Gothic Arch. Beyond its state-of-the-art curved roof, a gothic arch has been documented to resist extreme temperatures. It consists of either a galvanized pipe or a semicircular frame of groove and is usually covered with plastic.

Traditional or post and later. The most substantial designs to support the roof include embedded posts and rafters. This maximizes space utilization and provides efficient air circulation.

Freestanding. The increasing need for greenhouses that will be moved or removed gives rise to freestanding conservatories. As the name suggests, this type of greenhouse stands independently, allowing you to place or move it wherever you please. The material may be a group of hoops covered with plastic or a frame that runs on a rail or skid that will be moved with a tractor or wine. This sort is only right for greenhouses that only work during selected seasons such as summer or winter, and a freestanding greenhouse is your best bet as they are often removed and easily replaced again.

Materials and construction

A greenhouse construction may include glazing, framing, and laying the necessary foundations. Development is something you will want to do for as long as possible to avoid costly repair works. Choosing the most straightforward quality material to support your structure's durable and robust construction is your next big step.

After the foundation is in the right place, the primary content you work on is going to be the inspiration. Choosing a good foundation is the tricky part of building a greenhouse because it is critical to the component structure's stability and may be responsible for anchoring it in situ. You have got two options with the content, but the choice should tilt into your greenhouse and site dimensions as your budget.

Wood Choosing wood as a foundation is one of the economical ways to build a greenhouse. It is inexpensive and a stable foundation. The only common type is pressure-treated wood, which is an excellent choice for small conservatories. Resistant lumber such as cedar, redwood, and cypress are popular because they contain substances that prevent decay. For styles, railroad ties and platform construction are standard options for permanent drainage.

Such a foundation is highly recommended for solid cold climates as it helps eliminate the consequences of the lower freeze of the structure. A solid foundation provides a stable and secure base that will require less maintenance for the duration of your time. If you set it right. Building requires more experience and knowledge in pouring, leveling, and smoothing concrete. If you find this method more than a challenge, you will always try to get trained laborers for you.

Further note: In constructing a greenhouse foundation, it is necessary to create a lower level after removing soda and weeds. It is also essential to gauge your building code before building a foundation. You will need a selected permit, or there may also be a zoning law that prohibits foundations. Alternatively, there may also be a rule that allows you to give only one foundation.

Moving
forward, you will look at the materials that are occurring within the actual frame or 'skeleton' of your greenhouse. Frameworks are necessary to support the development of the structure. What cool material to use may depend on your chosen coverings or glazing? Heavy glazing requires a heavy frame. Here are some materials you might want to think about.

Wood This is often the most common material sought when it involves insulation and simple assembly. However, it is essential to choose redwood, cedar, or treated wood as other types of wood warfare can occur when moist or wet. With proper maintenance of the wood, you can live for a long time in a dry climate.

Compatibility. This low-maintenance material does not rust and has a tolerance to natural elements such as radiation and water. It will not be the strongest, but it provides an honest rigid look to the glass or polycarbonate casing.

Galvanized steel. Durable and cheap, galvanized steels require less morphology because the fabric has vital concrete components. However, there must be correct maintenance as the steel can wear and rust.

Polyvinyl chloride (PVC) plastic. The most straightforward benefit PVC plastic offers the restricted heat loss ideal for greenhouses that work during the winter season. They are lightweight, portable, and assembled directly. With this type of framing, you should take care in choosing a covering option. Thanks to its lightweight, it can only be ready to support a lightweight cover.

Odds and Ends

The difference between an average greenhouse and a greenhouse that will last you a lifetime is often determined by materials that add stability. Re-applying odds and ends is extra but will help your structure go the extra mile. The following are small additions you might want to think about to give your greenhouse the ultimate power.

Trussing. Long rods reinforced on the top rods to tie the ribs make the frame stronger. These rods run along all sides of the rib arches, which connect them together, so the vertical structure will be less likely to go up even with extreme wind and adverse weather.

Little beamer. These are added to the frame or foundation to give uniform stability. It is often of wood or metal.

Anchor. Cables that are either weighed or straight down are attached to surround the entire structure. This is usually done after glazing the greenhouse. With additional construction, the greenhouse can withstand high winds and storms.

Final walls. Additional end frames and doors secure a firm and are constructed for the rear greenhouse.

Greenhouse Covering is the final touch. As mentioned, choosing the type of materials for the panels should support the frame setup and the other way around. Additionally, it is also necessary to select glazing materials based on what percentage of layers are also required, which depends on the insulation amount.

Glass. Beyond its aesthetic appeal, glass glazing provides more light transmission than any commonly used glazing. It is a no brainer that Tumblr structures are fragile. However, repair issues that are mostly caused by projectiles such as hail are less likely.

Plastic. It is lighter and more versatile than glazing glass. They are available in larger pans, reducing drafts and making construction easier. Fiberglass is a type of plastic glazing that features a gel coat for UV protection, which retains heat better than glass. Polycarbonate is additionally a corrugated plastic that is almost glass-like transparent but longer than fiberglass. The cheapest option is a polyethylene film, which is usually employed by planters for seed initiation.

Greenhouse Floor

Whether you are raising your plants directly on the soil, on beds, or during hydroponic systems, greenhouse flooring should not be designed to serve only your plants. The ground is milled to ensure good drainage, insulate the greenhouse from the cold seeping ground, and prevent weeds and pests from coming in. While most of the environment is used for planting, the flooring is opted for from planting. I must be impressed. Way.

Soil. If the plants are grown directly on the earth, your greenhouse does not require a finished floor surface. Variations and compositions of clay beds are available, and therefore, the mixture you use will generally affect the expansion of your plants and the success of your greenhouse.

Further note: Old soil mixtures should never be reused explicitly as this method does not require raising the plants from the bottom up. Ground dwelling pests can easily break down and damage your plants. In cases where there are dead plants, they should be removed immediately from the greenhouse.

Stone, Gravel, and Pavers. These are ideal for floor type plants. Most commercial and residential greenhouses have erect beds directly on the ground, making stone, gravel, and pavers ideal for setup. This allows the root of the plant to grow deep in the soil below grade. Beds with pavers, flagstones, and crushed gravel are also favorite materials on the walkway.

Concrete When the planting strategy involves hydroponic or aquaponic systems, self-winding beds, or tables that require a flat surface, concrete is usually a moral choice. Although flat surfaces can also occur through gravel and stones, concrete has more advantages than convenience and maintenance. Carts rotate quickly with a durable and even surface. Besides, the concrete slab can be a concrete base that gives additional thermal mass, which helps maintain the specified temperature for your greenhouse.

Water quality and irrigation

Approximately a gallon of water mixed with nutrients is required daily to provide each plant. Analyzing the quality of greenhouse irrigation water is essential because the low rate is often responsible for slow and unhealthy growth and, in some cases, gradual death of plants. Alkalinity, pH, and soluble salt content are essential factors in determining the water's suitability to irrigate plants.

Further note: Reconstituted water and runoff or recycled water before being used for irrigation reduce the risk of disease-causing organisms, soluble salts, and organic chemicals that would be harmful to plants. The adjustments are as follows:

- Water for irrigation must have a pH between 5.0 and 7.0. Water with pH below 7.0 is called 'acidic,' and water with pH above 7.0 is called 'basic'; PH 7.0 is 7.0 neutral '.
- The pH level for vegetables and crops should be adjusted around 5.8 to 6.5.
- If the water source is fundamental, then seven million parts are enough, and add acids such as nitric, phosphoric, and sulfuric.
- If the water is acidic, but in seven, add one baser.

Water Methods

Irrigation of greenhouse plants is done through the application of water to the medium surface. This can be either through a drip tube or tape, employing a hand hose, overhead sprinkler, and boom. Other methods include pouring water through the container's rock bottom, utilizing a combination of sub-irrigation or delivery systems. Drinking water by hand is adequate but can be a chore, especially if you are performing on an outdoor scale. The media should not be saturated efficiently to take care of the plant until the next irrigation. A good range of water systems are often used to calculate the type and size of your greenhouse.

Sprinkler or overhead spray. Best for giant greenhouses that tolerate wet leaves. This irrigation system is like the saturation of natural rainfall. The water is distributed through the pipe system and then sprayed into the air through a sprinkler. The beginning of the water is small droplets that fall to the bottom. They also increase moisture levels in unplanned areas, which makes these unused sections ready for planting.

Misting and spray system. Works well on a large scale, used for propagation of seeds. Sprinkler works as an equal sprinkler but pours a more acceptable amount of water into the soil. Water pressure is right for transplanting water. It hydrates slowly and moistens the seeds without disturbing them. They are often in automated operation, which simplifies the method of cleaning water.

Micro drop or oyster duct system. The efficient water system for the size of any greenhouse. Alternatively known as a drip irrigation system, a micro drop allows water to slowly drip either onto the soil surface or directly into the plant's base area. The water moves through a network of valves, pipes, tubing, and emitters mounted on the media's surface or buried within it. The slow dripping nature of the system is less water wastage than escaping without letting the plants dry. Automated features include releasing water at intervals throughout the day.

Mat irrigation. Ideal for small greenhouses and novice gardeners. One method for quickly and easily watering plants is by placing them on seed capillary mats or self-watering trays. It is a tray with its water system coming from the reservoir. If you want to water it, you want to topmost water reserves, and so the trays on the capillary mat ooze the water. As the water system is drawn from moist ground, it forces the plants to grow deep roots, which will harvest more soil nutrients. This technique is perfect for transplanting freshly cut seeds and other plants that require constant moisture. Upstreaming the reservoir is usually done once every week, making rock bottom maintenance one of the options recommended for amateur growers.

The increasing demand for increased water irrigation promotes a more innovative water system that makes plant expansion consistent and uniform. Passionate producers are the primary to adopt the approach. Their investment allows them more free time while machines look out of their plants.

Automatic Irrigation System. Measures soil moisture and automatically activates or shuts down the water system, which is ideal for large projects. This method is automated or triggered, without which you do not need to turn anything on or off. Relying on set requirements, it operates on a timer and provides equal amounts of water to your plants. Automatic irrigation is beneficial for large greenhouses, where manually watering is time-consuming and inconvenient.

Solar-powered irrigation system. The simplest solution to water management with little dependence on the company's utilities, perfect for small greenhouses. Equipped with solar cells, and an environmentally friendly irrigation system does not require the use of electricity. This often occurs within drip irrigation connected to a non-pressurized water source that sucks through the water regularly throughout the day. This makes it wholly self-sufficient and hence the way forward for gardening.

Increase watering time for greenhouse plants

Since you are growing plants in an indoor location, where there is more control over environmental factors, determining when the correct watering time should support the greenhouse temperature, for cold and mildly cold temperatures, watering early within the day, therefore, serves as a trap for heat within the soil and touch to help the world around your plants stay warm as night approaches. Does. Meanwhile, in moist conditions, where there is a quick absorption of soil moisture, you will water at least twice each day. Just avoid watering at the top of the day because there is a bent that they do not dry up before sunlight. If the media is moist all night, the plants are often susceptible to fungal and bacterial diseases.

The temperature of the space predominantly affects the temperature of the water. A cold environment can have a substantially cold-water temperature, accompanied by a warm or hot climate. And you do not want to shock your plants with excessive calm or too much predation that can damage their tissues. Plants probably appreciate a pleasant 90–95 degrees Fahrenheit. During this case, the water system with an adjusted temperature range is beneficial. There are many other criteria to think about before planting, the planting method, the moisture level of the media, the slowness or condition of the plant, and exactly the type of plant you are handling.

Drainage solutions

The accumulation of even less irrigation water in the form of rainwater from the surface is of most concern for greenhouse operators, especially for ornamental growers. Plants may suffer from a lack of oxygen due to too much-wet soil. Also, wet floors are susceptible to accidents. On the opposite surface, rainwater can flow floodwater from the body inside the structure if the drainage is not applied correctly. Designing a correct system in and out of doors is essential to handle water sources' proper runoff.

The drainage inside the greenhouse ground bass can play an essential role in dealing with water accumulation. Start with a gravel or stone base six to eight inches below the ground. This foundation can offer you a defined area to fill with water when there are no finished surfaces or concrete floors. For drainage strategy, there are two primary methods widely used.

Surface drainage. The strategy is accomplished by shallow trenches or open drains that discharge larger and deeper waters. The surplus water is then facilitated through the constructed slope. A slope of eight inches per linear foot is usually quality.

The strategy involves removing water from the base zone. This is often done through deep open drains or buried pipe drains to enter and discharge through the line.

For your interiors, you will place a drain along sidewalks or post lines. This is going to cost you more but makes ground installation easier and floor drainage faster. Incorporating a soil mix with a good water holding capacity can be a neighborhood of drainage solution on your planting ground.

Peat moss. This soft, spongy, and fibrous structure is added to the overworked soil, which lacks the facility to expand its water holding capacity,

Perlite. What appears to be small foam balls is often seen during a potting medium that may be a perlite component. Round white soil rips the soil, enhances its water-retaining properties, and increases soil drainage.

Coarse sand. This rough graded material is employed to illuminate and ventilate the soil for a similar purpose of increasing soil drainage.

The driveways and chambers were built underground to provide water storage facilities for small greenhouses. In large structures, drains usually are attached and cause daylight. In some areas, greenhouse operators store water under either vinyl liner or sump to prevent fertilizer or pesticide from stepping into the water level. The water remains within the site until it dries.

Roof drainage

Designing a becomes an element that must be addressed explicitly at large greenhouses where there is an excess accumulation of water. Greenhouse gutters, downspouts, and drainpipes are often installed on the roof to handle excess water— Downspouts direct water into lateral pipes connected to a larger main. You want to be mindful of spacing because large gaps can end up in the water flowing above the gutter and into the greenhouse. The quality distance along the channels should be approximately 50 feet. It is recommended for larger installations to place it in the catch basin on top of each structure.

Another drainage solution to style a piping system that collects water and directs it to a pond or catchment area. A detention pond can prevent water from entering the greenhouse in the event of heavy rain. At the same time, it prevents flooding from its neighboring garden. The enormous amount of water on the pond continues slowly for several days. Additionally, it allows sedimentation, organic matter, and other pollutants to drain out before releasing water.

Further note: There are laws and regulations that govern water discharge into another person's property. In some places that are covered by the Inland Wetland Code, permits are required to discharge water in protected areas such as marshes, protected ponds, and marshes.

Environmental control greenhouses can provide their operators with the opportunity to control the space's environment, regardless of the weather outside. Better control means that you will host the broadest range of plants and support almost any plant type. Relying on their commitment and budget.

Many climate control methods equip complex systems with heating, cooling, and ventilation systems.

Greenhouses are created by heating plants that shelter greenhouses with solar heat traps and circulating air to create an artificial environment that will sustain life when the outdoor temperature is exactly right. The strategy may work for a one-hundred-gram solar heated greenhouse. But in operating greenhouses with cool climates with little or no supplemental heat, operators come up with creative ways to expand energy efficiency in addition to orienting the conservatory towards the sun.

Insulation. Greenhouses often use insulation costs, including glazing and floor levels, to accelerate energy efficiency while heating costs. Window, transparent plastic cover, layers of thermal screen, and ground the base are among the preferred options.

Cold frame. Built from bottom to bottom, transparent roof enclosures protect plants from extreme cold. The transparent top allows sunlight to escape in and avoid heat through convection.

Thermal mass. In rooms with little exposure to sunlight, thermal mass storage is impervious to collecting and storing the sun's energy through a metal metal-drum. The metal transfers the heat of the sun to the water. The water then brings the heat back to the entire greenhouse. Other thermal materials that are used with a similar method are plastic tubes and concretes.

Heating System. Heating using light fixtures such as radiant lamps hanging on plants is one way to offer the necessary heat. Combined with the soil heating cable under the plants, they create a warm environment. A 220-volt circuit electric fire can also serve as artificial heat. There are also solar heaters in the form of heating fans designed explicitly for greenhouses.

Greenhouse

Cooling the Cooling methods are commonly used in most places and in the summer height where the recent and steamy detour is too much for plants to handle. Additionally, some plants require a cooling environment to grow and when a cooling system is available. Each cooling method has its limitations and business, which one must balance and surround.

Shading. Where there is exposure to strong sunlight, shading can protect plants from burning by reducing sunlight. Shed clothing is effective in reducing temperatures up to 10 degrees. Roll-up screens, wood aluminum, vinyl plastic shedding, or paint-on materials may also be used for shade plants—the tradeoff required to be balanced between a low temperature and some required radiation being blocked.

Fans and Vents. Excess heat is usually trapped within fossil greenhouses. Natural circulation of air is often done through ventilation and fanning. The roof and side vents can create an exemplary airflow, while the roof and exhaust fans create the necessary movement to cool overhead plants. The only drawback with fans in dry and hot places is that dry foliage and planting can occur on media if dry.

Evaporative cooling. As the water evaporates, it increases the humidity level within the air. Evaporative cooling uses the natural relationship between humidity, water, and air temperature for that cooling effect. The amount of cooling achieved through this method depends on the proportion of water often evaporating and the relative humidity or amount of water already contained within the air. This method gives rise to evaporative coolers that automatically transform hot air into cold air using the evaporated water method. Another system developed through this method is the fogging system that generates small droplets of water within the range of 10–20, cools, and provides an inexpensive ratio.

Soaking in water Wet hardening surfaces can effectively soothe hot humidity. A mist system is often used to deliver water precipitation to an air space or walkway. But when the mist has its cool benefits, you need to keep in mind that wetting a cover can cause plant diseases and damage to fruits.

Further note: You will quickly feel that the greenhouse's indoor temperature is hot or cold for the plants to survive. However, in some situations, you cannot always believe the feeling of your stomach. Through thermometers and other climate-measuring devices, you will monitor your greenhouse's exact heat or cold temperature to ensure optimal growing conditions for your plants.

Greenhouse plant

Within the number of pollinators of the nature of birds, bees, and butterflies. An equivalent barrier that protects plants from adverse growing conditions may also prevent pollinators from doing their job. So how does pollination occur inside a pollination structure? A tactile intervention can ensure that plants are often successfully pollinated, even in protected greenhouses.

Manual pollution. This will take some time to touch, but the pollen comes out slowly by tapping the flowers. Disturbing flowers from male to female plants distribute pollen with each bloom.

Device pollination. If you cannot fit manual pollination into your program, you will use a battery-powered pollination tool. This is still what you need as an operator, but these tools speed up work.

Bee pollination. Bees are naturally pollinated. Some bumblebee pollinators are often raised for pollination purposes. You will buy a box or hive of bees and place them in your greenhouse if you can provide supplemental food sources for these pollutants further.

Note further: During high humid environments, use fans to dry the plants before pollination. High humidity levels can cause pollinators to coexist, making pollination efforts unsuccessful. Also, it is best to pollinate the plants between 10 am and 3 pm.

Ensuring a pest and disease-free environment

Good plant health and environmental control are the first defense mechanisms against pests and diseases that disturb your greenhouse plants. But in some instances, aphids, whiteflies, and mites are often difficult to control due to resistance to most pesticides. However, you will still prevent and eliminate pests by taking preventive measures and actions later.

In the primary sign of disturbance, mechanical controls such as vacuuming, squashing, and washing are essential for biological control.
If pests still grow and multiply, then it is best to use soap or pepper spray.
Yellow sticky traps are also effective against white sticky.
Neem and horticultural oils manage the early stages of pest development, while pyrethroids can kill adult pests.
Meanwhile, the fungal disease is usually the best disease problem for greenhouse plants. A similar humid temperature that favors many plants can promote these diseases, which is another reason to supply adequate ventilation.

Monitoring and balancing the distance between plants and moisture levels are ways to prevent fungal problems. If the disease had already affected the plants, apply preventive sprays to isolate the affected area and isolate or quarantine the plant. If the problem still occurs, it is best to eliminate sick plants because fungi cause organisms to mold.

Safety and luxury security is one of the main concerns within the greenhouse, especially when it involves electricity. Electric shocks are particularly likely to splatter in greenhouses where you search for plants. Avoid wet heaters and another electrical wiring. A safety check should be administered regularly, and special attention should be taken to deal with lightning to prevent any possible contact between the water and electrical connections.

For flammable materials and gas-fired appliances, keep them away from the heater. It is a simple idea to install a smoke detector and extinguisher in the event of a bush fire. Proper safety is additionally paramount for regular working activities. Sometimes, work-related injuries are often up to your exertion, but it also entails correct maintenance. The repair work required to avoid accidents, whether on equipment, interiors, or materials, should be corrected immediately.

On the opposite hand, rest is required to perform fully well-tended plants and other work necessary for a productive greenhouse. For example, eatery access to a conservatory may be better, especially when maintenance issues arise. Comfort also comes into play if you combine gardening with leisure. Some include a mini "living space" where they will just sit and relax while observing their plants or reading their favorite books. But whatever you envision your greenhouse, both safety and luxury should consider the commitment of that greenhouse.

Budget Plans

After studying the many ideas needed to plan a greenhouse, you are ready to go. If there is no money, then allocating a budget will not be an excessive amount of work. In cases where one is tight on account, carefully giving and dividing expenses among materials, construction labor can be a time well spent. But you all have that cash to spare, and it still knows how to get some tips and ways to save money in building and maintaining your greenhouse. The trick is to allocate the budget to the requirements before 'excess goods' occur. Your budget will determine what you will do and put it in the greenhouse. The latter factors are necessary to get into your account list. Also, we have selected their estimated costs for a better and better budget allocation for you.

The Greenhouse size greenhouse
The larger, the more material required. If you want to avoid expensive expenses, then it is necessary to think about how big you want your conservatory to be.

Essential start (cost: approx. $ 240). Very affordable, a 6'x8 'enclosure structure and greenhouse kit have everything you want to get started. Plumbing and electronics are not included in the estimate. This is often an ideal setup for moderate climates.

Experienced producers (cost: $ 3,500– $ 7,000). The 12'x12 'greenhouse is covered with a common roof for more dedicated growers. Many additional costs include motivation, running plumbing and electrical systems.

Serious producers (cost: $ 12,000- $ 25,000). A 500 to 1000 square foot is the size for an average greenhouse structure that sometimes has all the amenities, including an automatic water system, feeders, and light increases. Flooring usually goes with systems of concrete poured

Material options

That will enter your design, the most significant impact on your budget. Quality material is often expensive, which is why people stay far away from it. This is good for a bargaining officer but confirms that you are not skipping the standard required to build that strong greenhouse.

Cover Material:

- Glass - About $ 2.50 Sq. Ft.
- Polyethylene - about $ 0.12 per square foot
- filament - about $ 72.00 per 6 × 8 panel
- polycarbonate - about $ 55.00 per 8 × 4 sheet

Framing material:

- wood, cedar - about $ 1.00 per linear foot
- Steel -abba $ 2.50 per linear foot

Excavation:

- Concrete - Approximately $ 10.00texture and drainage, and

- per square foot of pavers with about $ 8.00 to $ 11.00 per square foot -
- electricity - about 0.75 to $ 3.00 per square foot

Construction labor costs

Lighting, heating ventilation, and air-con (HVAC) of small Greenhouses with an easy setup will not drag along. For large projects, it will be difficult for even experienced professionals to handle these installments and other construction needs. For this reason, you will have to contact licensed contractors to request a bid or bid for the work. Hiring these contractors can be half to cool down the total cost of your project.

Operating costs and maintenance expenses do not stop after the development of the greenhouse. Operating costs include plant production, seeds, substrate, pesticides, and supplemental plant nutrients. Another introductory price is that utility bills such as HVAC and irrigation systems. Before investing within construction, it is known to check the price of electricity in your area. If you are planning to operate a greenhouse, it is crucial to evaluate work expenses.

Building and zoning permits

Some large greenhouse installations such as foundations, HVAC, irrigation, and systems may require installation permits and must be done by licensed individuals (as previously mentioned). Additionally, 'outbuilding' or 'farm building' greenhouses may require building and zoning permits prior to development. If you are going to build a greenhouse, it is recommended to consult your local code enforcement officer in the classification. If the greenhouse can be a safe place for its owners and operators, the purpose of those permits is to gauge.

Zoning Permit. Suppose your community is under a zoning code. In that case, authorities may, for example, require you to have a greenhouse plan that shows the status of the greenhouse in terms of property boundaries and other neighboring structures. It can be side, back, or front lines and can be determined by your community's rules and regulations. Regulations also include accessories and, therefore, the size of the building under this permit.

Building permit. In some cases, after meeting the zoning requirements, one may also be required to request a license. A county department office usually issues this permit. The code addresses structural integrity and, therefore, the physical appearance of your greenhouse.

Further note: In some communities, an enclosure house is not considered a permanent structure and does not require a permit. In others, the owner must supply an engineer seal that certifies that the ring house meets all code standards. However, each community has its own rules and laws. In the end, it is still sensible to watch with your local code. The last item you want to get or build a greenhouse that does not meet the local code because failure to comply with it can result in costly fines or, even worse, the demolition of your significant investment.

CHAPTER 4: GREENHOUSE ENVIRONMENT

Your crop production can be significantly accelerated using greenhouse environment systems or automation. This type of environmental control keeps the greenhouse stable to supply the best conditions that are most favorable for maximum yield.

The ability of a plant to grow and grow depends mainly on photosynthesis. Within sunlight's presence, the plant makes sugar by mixing CO_2 and water, which are then used for the growth and production of flowers/fruits.

Management of the greenhouse environment is directed towards optimizing the photosynthetic process within plants and the plant's ability to use light at its maximum efficiency.

Greenhouse Lighting Control

There are tons more carefully received than greenhouse lighting. Producers looking for sufficient light for his or her greenhouse should consider the following three factors: what kind of crop is being grown, what time of year it is, and the way too much sunlight is coming out.

Greenhouses typically require six hours of direct or full-spectrum lighting every day. If this cannot be done naturally, supplemental lighting should be included. Supplementary lighting is the use of multiple, high-intensity artificial lights for crop growth and yield. Hobbyists want to use them to grow and extend the growing season, while commercial growers use them to spice up productivity and profits.

Producers have an excellent array of lighting options to choose from, so it is essential to know different lighting styles' nuances. Again, greenhouses become easier to manage with environmental controls that will be scheduled and monitored.

Humidity control

As plants begin to increase their growth rate, you may want to gradually reduce moisture to encourage evaporation, allowing more water to flow to the plant. Because the plant consumes more water, long cells replenish nutrients and deliver nutrients to growing parts of the plant.

Moisture should also be observed because if it gets too high in the greenhouse, the plant leaves have a better chance of getting wet. Unfortunately, soggy leaves are one of the simplest ways to ensure an epidemic of mycosis or mildew. Vegetable diseases such as fungal pathogens or mildew are common greenhouse culprits. Seeing and controlling the greenhouse environment means better internal control.

Ventilation and fan control is other easy thanks to venting use to help regulate temperature and humidity. With the use of racks and wings and ventilation control, you will trigger the greenhouse vent to open at a group temperature if it starts to get too hot.

Also, we measure the ratio (the amount of water vapor present in the air expressed as a percentage of the volume required for saturation.) Which can also be reduced by opening the vents. Hot, dry air and not wet.

We can also trigger horizontal airflow fans with greenhouse control systems. These improve air circulation and help to expel moisture from the air. It is necessary to increase the greenhouse temperature for correct equilibrium.

With appropriate greenhouse temperature and humidity sensors, this is often controlled through our greenhouse automation computer. This can help you see and regulate moisture and temp levels more effectively. Our producers have approved greenhouse environmental control software so that all stations remain in moderation.

Carbon dioxide or CO2 control

Distributing much CO2 to your plants is essential for healthy plant growth.

Plants take carbon from the air as an essential component of photosynthesis. CO2 enters the plant through the opening of the foramen by the method of diffusion.

CO2 increases productivity through improved plant growth and overall health. Some methods to increase productivity during CO2 include earlier flowering, fruiting more, and longer growth cycles.

By acquiring more technical mathematics here, pure photosynthesis increases as CO_2 levels rise from 340–1,000 ppm (per million parts) except for the bulk of greenhouse crops.

Most crops suggest that for any level of active photosynthetic radiation (PAR), increasing the CO_2 level to 1,000 ppm will increase photosynthesis by about 50% at ambient CO_2 levels.

Stay within the internal control guidelines with our Greenhouse Climate System to control the CO_2 range properly.

Air temperature control air temperature
It is increasing the speed of photosynthesis to some extent. However, above 85 degrees, plants enter photoreception. Plants that do not adapt to growing will start to fade.

Also, suppose you do not match the upper air temperature with high levels of CO_2 and light intensity. In that case, your plants are going to do more photorespiration than photosynthesis, which can have a significant impact on the health of your plants.

At a particular point, enzymes will not function independently and may decompose, and your plants will not establish a healthy metabolism. Overall balance with our greenhouse temperature system is essential.

Regular irrigation and fertilizer - Fertility control
We want a daily irrigation and nutrient formula for crops within the greenhouse. This is often the case in today's large commercial operations where fission automation can not only help but better help all other farms.

Fertilization continuously applies a significant amount of water and fertilizers through the irrigation system. The supply of essential nutrients to crops helps in maintaining yields better.

Fertigation is particularly useful in the case of drip irrigation. Water and hence nutrients are directly absorbed into the roots with our automated breeding equipment—improvement in speed, growth, and quality of crops.

This system may be a more rational use of water and fertilizers. I think that respecting the environment and reducing environmental impact are things that we will all get out of. We will also use the Greenhouse Water Recycling System to ensure that your crops are safe.

CHAPTER 5: ESSENTIAL GREENHOUSE EQUIPMENT

Any professional greenhouse producer knows that adding in some greenhouse furnishings and systems is extremely important to achieve a maximum year-round growing environment.

Not only do these glasshouses offer you the possibility to grow several of your favorite plants, fruits, and vegetables, they also enable you to develop all of these throughout the year. However, buying a greenhouse structure is just the beginning of it, as there are many accessories that you will have to consider buying. These are eleven of the essential items available for your greenhouse.

Greenhouse heating is usually, two types of heating systems involve a greenhouse, a central system, and a unit system. What you want will depend on the spread of things, including what kind of plants you must grow and, therefore, the greenhouse size. Each heating plant has its unique advantages, so there are disadvantages, so you must research adequately to meet your special gardening needs.

Greenhouse ventilation

To take care of the right greenhouse environment, you should invest during ventilation. You will choose between an automatic or manual system. Automated systems provide convenience because an automatic timer will open greenhouse vents when a particular temperature is reached. In some cases, a lover may also be active. Manual systems assume that a person is opening them by hand and is generally only fair to use in considerably basic greenhouses. Adequate ventilation will also reduce the appearance of mildew and mold.

Plant fertilizer

No greenhouse plant would be complete without the supply of plant fertilizer to aid healthy growth. While standard fertilizers are relatively cheap, expensive organic fertilizers are growing in popularity. Not only are organic options good for plants, but they also help protect the environment.

Greenhouse pest control is essential for every gardener to protect their plants from pests that fly and fly. Therefore, no greenhouse is complete without an open insect system. There are many environmentally friendly versions for people who inadvertently harm their plants or the environment because of standard pesticides. An easy trap will help keep out flies and other small insects.

Greenhouse Watering System Release
Water wands small droplets of water during direct mist on plants. These wands work on timers so that you will have peace of mind about your plant's water system. Drip systems are often larger and provide more significant amounts of water. A drip system also uses a timer and is perfect for an outdoor area of water.

Greenhouse Irrigation System

If you have found a live water system, you must also implement an irrigation system to request additional wastewater from the greenhouse. Virtually all systems combine a uniform fashion with just the shape to separate them. All these work in a delegated area by taking the path of excess water from the plants, which is usually the soil of your garden.

Greenhouse staging and shelving system
mounting racks are great location savers for small greenhouses. They are designed to protect plants from harsh weather and accidental knocks. For smaller structures, greenhouse shelving units are often used as two-tier freestanding units, three-tier freestanding units, or four-tier freestanding units. These units are easy to assemble, and therefore, it is vital to shelve to keep the greenhouse clean and organized.

Lighting

Lighting units provide essential lighting for you to add a greenhouse once there is little natural sunlight. Companies must be waterproof and have a safety travel-switch that will automatically stop the flow of electricity if the company is compromised by inclement weather, water, or anything else. Greenhouse lighting is essential for winter gardening when hours are lacking in daylight.

Digital Thermometer

A thermometer can also be a little helpful, but it is one of the most important when it involves greenhouse gardening. Because some plants thrive at certain temperatures, a thermometer will help ensure that the proper temperature is achieved and if the temperature drops below a safe range. Plants do not run well in the weather, and frost can kill them quickly, so a thermometer helps ensure that your greenhouse temperature is controlled.

Greenhouse Covering

Everyone knows that plants need sunlight to grow, but not everyone knows that excessive amounts of sunlight are often harmful to their growth. Clothes sheds fit on the windows and can be pulled down when daylight is healthy to give the plants some shade. Shades will also help prevent the temperature from becoming uncomfortable.

Cleaning kits

Unique microfiber fabrics and demister spray greenhouses are essential cleaning items. Using them together helps eliminate condensation on greenhouse windows, which reduces the chances of mold and mildew.

CHAPTER 6: USING SPACE EFFECTIVELY

Find out the available in your greenhouse if you are making fair use of the space use. With small greenhouse kits, every bit of space is counted. Therefore, you should ensure that you maximize the entire area in your greenhouse.

One way to try to do this is to use a rolling bench often or insist on a little greenhouse kit like the Selex 8 ft x 8 ft Garden Master or Onion-sized Riga 2 that has pre-built shelving. These kits typically maximize mounting space quite efficiently.

Crop programs and planning

Where possible, try to use your greenhouse to its fullest potential. Believe what season you are in and are starting to grow plants that will withstand cool temperatures quickly. Get an idea of the plants you want to overgrow. Then schedule everything from sowing to harvesting so that you can use the greenhouse space to full capacity. Some plants take less time to prepare for harvesting, for example, spinach and radish. Once you cut those people, you will use the opportunity to do something else or its equivalent, and it is up to you.

Planting of Plants

Depending on the time of year, you will start your plants inside your small greenhouse and plant them in your garden. This not only saves space inside your greenhouse but gives you an excellent start to surface weather.

Transplants are often more resistant to pests and other pests because they are more developed and more extensive when you first plant them in your garden. Birds that choose their seed outside your garden beds have no problem.

Greenhouse Layering and Staging

Can crops be leveled? Sometimes, adding a second crop under your first planting can work brilliantly until the plants' germinate. For example, you are using forests above crops that take longer to germinate.

Greenhouse staging is highly fashionable for gardeners. This gives many areas for your seedling and plants. It also maximizes vertical mounting space. By staging your crops, you create more shaded areas under benches. This would be beneficial for species that develop fully under low light conditions. Kale and other leafy vegetables work only fine in shady places.

Zoning Dividing

Your greenhouse into zones will help you use the space most efficiently. As mentioned above, you will use shades for zoning. You would consider counting your crops in what proportion they have heat. Transplant crops that grow only in hot temperatures on the verge of heat sources. Then, add a touch to your cold-tolerant crops that are separated from the heat. In this way, you have found optimal conditions to grow your crops faster and more efficiently.

Zoning your greenhouse is not only for increased efficiency but also for the organization. Imagine benches and shelves. Planning different areas for your plants will reduce clutter and can keep pests away from the garden. Keep the stuff you usually use in one place, and you will not waste precious time on them. Planning for zoned locations in your garden is a great idea to ensure that you are getting to the most critical place.

Hooks, hanging pots, and other greenhouse accessories to maximize space during a small greenhouse helps
Vertical gardening uses smaller spaces to maximize them. Use hooks, spirals, top shelves, or hanging utensils from the ceiling or sideways. You will either use it for growing, for drying herbs, or for storing gardening tools. Be inexperienced. Clip together gardening gloves or packets of seeds and hang them on the walls with hooks.

Hanging pots add a stimulating design to your greenhouse if placed in high areas. For the convenience of use, you will use the plant caddy hook. You will quickly reduce your pots with the form to take care of your plants.

CHAPTER 7: GROWING IN YOUR GREENHOUSE

Growing in happiness every year as the autumnal equinox passes through us, decreasing rapidly to a noticeable degree day by day. It becomes too cold and dark in many areas for anything within the region to grow by the solstice. But greenhouse growers are ready to make tomatoes, lettuce, eggplant and pepper seeds, or other carefully selected vegetables, herbs, and flowers. Transplanting can also be initiated or transplanted to a heated or unheated greenhouse or hoop house, counting the latitude, harvest, and many additional variables unique to the greenhouse grower's operations.

The apparent reason to grow greenhouse vegetables, flowers, and herbs is to keep crops with you at the time of year, as they cannot be grown outdoors. Outside, tomatoes, cucumbers, peppers, eggplants, lettuce, basil, and other vegetables command higher prices in some markets.

However, it is vital to notice that the value of winter production of warm-weather crops such as tomatoes is exceptionally high, so prepare it to leap on just one occasion, when you get a market and value that Heating your return on investment is going to be your highest cost, after labor. And plan to remain in production during the winter months at the very least. You will also have to provide supplemental lighting - especially during extended spans of overcast weather. Suppose you have never tried to grow greenhouse vegetables in winter. In that case, you should do an excellent deal of preliminary research to see if they are often profitable for you, given your climate, greenhouse composition, and fuel costs. Fortunately, there are many freely available resources to help you calculate costs and potential returns. An online look for the Greenhouse Tomato Enterprise budget, for example, will return a long list of references to state your research. Search for people published by your regional universities and cooperative extension agencies.

A useful tool called Virtual Grower is out there, through the USDA, to predict heating costs. This free software program prompts the user to enter information such as the nearest meteorological observation post (from where the average weather conditions are calculated), the type of greenhouse structure, structure conditions, heating plants, and fuel prices.

For the time being, a broad rule of thumb for an early grower in the northern half of the US or Canada should not be imposed in a greenhouse until 15 February, as earlier low light conditions make the crop a risky venture. Experienced growers and southern growers, however, can often produce all winter. As of mid-February, many crops are grown with only minimal heat and still provide a month or more of growth than farm crops.

If you have found a market where you will sell vegetables in the spring, greenhouse production is often profitable, especially with early field crops. For example, you can grow spinach ready in April, but it is hardly enough to fill a market trend. If, however, you will also bring Lectica Sativa capitata from the heated greenhouse, and can take arugula, radish, and carrots from the unheated enclosure, you can put it on an honest display. Alternatively, believe in Mother's Day occasions: greenhouse tomatoes, cucumbers, chopped flowers, and flower baskets hang, and there is a plethora of strawberries, plus a full range of spring vegetables.

The extension of the season is just one of the benefits of growing greenhouses. Protected crops are no less suitable to be damaged by wind, rain, and hail, so the percentage of marketed products is higher. The yield is generally higher if you will provide optimal conditions for each crop. Greenhouses protect crops from many diseases, especially those that splash soil and splash on plants during rain. And greenhouse crops can also be protected from common area pests. Of course, greenhouse crops have their particular problems, such as foliage, aphids, and whiteflies, so vigilance is necessary.

Greenhouse vegetables, herbs, and flowers are often grown in three central systems: in-ground soil culture, container culture, and hydroponics. The primary is easiest for beginners because the requirements for water and fertilization are not as precise. Growing in containers, however, has the advantages of doing any weeding and soil-less diseases. Therefore, the determining factor may be the type of greenhouse that you have. If you have found a transplant house with a concrete or gravel floor, you will need to grow in containers such as bags, bulb crates, or large utensils. If you have found an earthen floor, you will choose which system to use.

In either case - unless you are using hydroponics - drip irrigation has been suggested to do back labor, improve water stability, and problems caused by overhead watering such as soil spills and wet leaves. Stop Plastic mulch may also be used to prevent weeds while preserving soil moisture. An inner layer of row cover held above the crops by hoops may also be used to keep the soil warm without increasing fuel use.

Tomatoes, cucumbers, peppers, and brinjals need to be trailed on the twine's vertical length. The wine is often paired with trellis with the taper, an instrument that wraps a versatile band with stem and trellis string. Roller hooks provide for maximum timesaving, space-preserving during a lower - & - skeletal system. Other greenhouse crops like basil and chopped flowers can be held upright with a horizontal trailing system such as the Horton ova netting. To learn about the various crop support tools and accessories available, take the time to pick up the design for your application best.

You can grow almost anything during a greenhouse, but this protected space is prime land - with careful different options, you will make maximum profit and produce crops that are not best for you.

Tomato is the number-one greenhouse crop grown within the US, probably because demand is high and consistent. Cucumbers are the second-largest greenhouse crop, followed by lettuce and salad mix. Greenhouse papers are also prevalent within the US and offer diverse options, though more precisely, their cultural requirements. Microgreens, too, are in stable year-round demand and provide many benefits, including short turnarounds, relative ease in growing, tremendous diversity, and appreciable ROI.

Among herbs, basil is often grown before and after greenhouses, and there is a similar demand for it. Tender perennial herbs such as Rosemary and Thyme are usually kept as mother plants within greenhouses, then propagated to be sold as container plants in late winter or culinary cut herbs in spring. Strawberries are another valuable greenhouse crop and can be grown in hanging containers to empty the floor space for other crops.

Whatever crops you choose, variety selection is critical to greenhouse success. The varieties are almost identified for greenhouse production for several reasons. They have increased resistance to common diseases or will grow better under low light conditions of the greenhouse. In cucumbers, many greenhouse varieties are parthenocarpy, meaning they do not require insect pollination for line fruit - and gynecology, meaning that all flowers are female, yielding a better yield because each flower has one Can show fruit. Remember the red greenhouse symbol on our website and next to the various names on our list.

CHAPTER 8: SCHEDULING PLANTS OF YEAR-ROUND GROWING

From Year to Year How does your backyard greenhouse supply food throughout the year? There are two fundamental factors to consider when planning your greenhouse planting schedule: temperature and day length.

Day length is arguably the most critical factor when determining when to plant in your greenhouse. If you are not using supplemental lighting, it will be essential for you to understand the average length of the day for the entire year in your area.

At the beginning of February, we are in Colorado when our day length begins to succeed 10 hours per day, which is usually enough daylight to germinate. And in the middle of November comes the time when our days are reduced by 10 hours, and the plant growth slows down considerably. The plant will still survive throughout the winter but will typically enter a semi-hibernation. If you plant your winter garden adequately, the plants are nearing maturity by the top of November, and you will be ready to slowly prune off all the winter from semi-dormant plants, even supplemental lights without even.

The temperature inside your greenhouse and therefore also within will affect many micro-climate increases. The coldest parts of your conservatory will usually be on the verge of your greenhouse glazing and right next to your vents. This is where you want to make your cold-hardy vegetables like spinach and bananas in winter. The hottest part of your greenhouse will usually be along the north wall, where the sun is reflected and kills nearby plants. By planning your planting schedule to suit the length of the day, the location of your plant, the supported temperature, and choosing the appropriate crops and varieties, you will be ready to harvest vegetables throughout the year.

There may be a rough planting calendar that we use for our location near Denver, Colorado, at the latitude of about 40 degrees.

February:
As we move towards the equinox, the days begin to get bigger. We are in Colorado; February marks the time when there is sufficient daylight (about 10 hours a day) to seed new crops without using auxiliary lights.

Begin your first spring round of cold-tolerant crops (lettuce, kale, radish, beets, carrots, peas, etc.).

Start growing crops of warm-loving, long-season vegetables within the greenhouse (tomatoes, peppers, brinjals, etc.). These crops typically take 100–150 days to mature, and that they do not tolerate the weather, so when they grow and ripen their fruits, they are given the longest possible time in a warm climate. You will start these crops in your greenhouse and transplant them outside after the temperature is above 55 degrees at night. Otherwise, you can keep them in your greenhouse for a long time in summer and growing in autumn.

March / April:
Near the vernal equinox, daylight and plants begin to grow more rapidly within the greenhouse. Start warm weather crops with short days to maturity (beans, basil, cucumbers, squash).

Start cutting from your first round of cold-tolerant crops and continue planting cold-tolerant, growing crops to grow them quickly.

May:

Long days and warm nights develop amazingly fast in your greenhouse.

You will probably harvest tons from crops such as lettuce, kale, spinach, and peas.

Suppose you have started transplanting within the greenhouse. In that case, you will now begin to planting cold-tolerant transplants (broccoli, cauliflower, cabbage) because already plunging temperatures are consistently above 45 degrees, and warm-weather transplants are outside. (Tomato, Chili), Brinjal) Once already dark, temperatures are always above 55 degrees.

June / July:

This is usually a warm-up time for the greenhouse, which counts the cooling systems you have received. Your warm crops, such as peppers, eggplants, beans, and tomatoes, are going to be incredibly happy within the greenhouse, but you will still need to confirm that they are warm and that you get proper ventilation, which you got enough moisture for. It is to protect plants from overdose and transplanting.

August / September:

August and September are usually the time to start planting your winter garden. November through November, the length of the day such plants will grow very slowly without supplemental lighting.

Your goal with a winter garden is to plant enough that most plants are on the verge of reaching maturity by November or December. As plant growth slows, your crops will enter a semi "hibernation," and you will be ready to harvest slowly even in winter without seeing entirely new growth.

It is time to maneuver some room plants inside the greenhouse for the winter before your area's primary frost. Sour, figs, peppers, and tomatoes that are in the pot outside can avoid winter in the pool inside the greenhouse. We have seen that pepper plants are more than three years old and are still producing fruits.

October:

Days are getting shorter. You are already planting your winter garden, but October can still provide enough light to start crops with noticeably short cycles (such as radishes that mature only 20-30 days) or start such crops. The ones you decide to do within the bus are late winter / early spring, knowing that they will grow very slowly in winter.

Hardy vegetables such as spinach, lettuce, and kale will now typically have time to grow and grow smaller plants, overwinter, and grow as fast as the day in February. The taste of winter and early spring vegetables is sweeter than at other times of the year as the vegetables begin to store sugars in their cell walls to protect them from frost damage.

November / December / January:

The time of rest and lethargy before the last season begins again. You will still harvest slowly from mature plants, pulling bud leaves, digging carrots and beets, or cutting spinach. Now is also the time to prune your fruit trees, read seed catalogs, and plan for next year's garden.

If you prefer to use complementary lighting, greenhouse development is not hindered during this point. Leafy greens and root vegetables will thrive in your winter greenhouse with a touch of added light. We have also seen that greenhouses grow warm-season crops in winter, such as tomatoes and peppers, with supplemental light if the greenhouse night temperature can be below 62 degrees. Because a Ceres greenhouse reflects crop light away from its north, east, and west walls, we are ready to use less complimentary light for more robust winter growth.

CHAPTER 9: HYDROPONICS IN A GREENHOUSE

If the primary "agricultural revolution" started in humans, when humans began growing crops in the dirt, then maybe another time we start getting them entirely out of the ground.

We are talking, of course, about hydroponics - the revolutionary, soil-free method of growing crops, vegetables, which has given off a replacement wave of happiness within the agricultural industry.

A significant reason for all interest in hydroponics: the latest systems are designed to increase profits and reduce long-term costs. Whether it is from the conservation of resources or the removal of traditionally time-consuming manual labor, the producers of tomorrow have tons to love about hydroponic technology.

Here is a look at some of the critical ways hydroponics helps growers increase operating costs in the long run and why it would be urging your development operations to be found with hydroponic systems.

1. Improve water efficiency

Typically, a grower working with plants in a conventional dirt medium can expect to lose a large portion of the water they cover the plants for runoff. This can not only cause leaching and contamination of the local water supply, but it also represents a loss in operating profits that has traditionally been unavoidable.

Because hydroponics eliminates the need for planting within the dirt or within the ground and uses water themselves primarily as a growing medium, these systems leave behind water runoff for growers and increase water efficiency after the season. It makes it easy for everyone. All the water in your hydroponic system is present during a closed-loop course, which means that almost every drop is employed to the full extent without losing gravity or other thirsty plants.

2. Maximize profitable space.

One of the essential complaints we hear from growers is that they struggle to find that balance between "too much-wasted land" and "too little space for plants to flourish." It is often difficult to increase the standard unproductive space present in many traditional development works and realize that sweet spot in terms of profits-per-square feet.

Therefore, with their compact spacing and highly efficient use of horizontal ground space, hydroponic systems provide a severe boost to square-foot productivity within your greenhouse or high tunnel structure, favoring uncontrolled, condensed growing areas. By eliminating that waste space, an equal amount of ground space is used to produce growers to supply more significant and better crops.

3. Reduced pests and diseases

In almost every traditional growing operation, the soil is one of the primary vectors for pests, diseases, and other harmful pathogens to succeed in your plants. Whether it is thanks to water runoff from an affected area or just a natural rhythm of soil health, growing underground will almost always expose plants to the risk of disease and pests - while hydroponics can, on the opposite hand, help at all Is other.

A hydroponic system can be a closed system, meaning that there should be no easy entry or exit point for pests, diseases, mold, or other pathogens, even to get your plants in the first place.

If you and your growers maintain industry-standard cleaning and hygiene practices between plantations, your crops should remain pest-free much more quickly than crops grown within the soil. Severe savings on pest prevention means and significantly lower the risk of harm to disease or contamination.

4. Needs of any wedding

Pests and diseases are not the only invaders who need the benefit of your growing crops. When planted in soil, weeds can quickly creep into your crop beds. Which will eat up time, labor, and a spotlight, which you would not otherwise need to empty.

Because hydroponic systems are soil-free and closed, weeds will have no chance of settling your crops in the first place. You will spend less time worrying about weeds and other biological invaders, who will harvest your crops and ensure that your produce is as full and delightful as possible.

5. Grow More Profitable Plants Indoors

When you prefer to grow, it often means choosing only those crops that are likely to achieve your area. For example, not all soils are right for growing grapes, while climatic conditions and temperatures can make it difficult to refer to essential crops, especially in cold or storm-prone areas.

Hydroponics, on the other hand, do not believe outdoor conditions function correctly. This means that with the proper hydroponic setup, you will set your sights on growing more profitable crops than ever before, expanding yourself to that profit-per-square-foot, and reducing wasted energy When it takes time.

6. Four Seasons Farming
For an exceptionally long time, farmers are forced into a changing season and a fluctuating season when deciding when and where to grow their crops. Northern climates or regions are likely to experience storms, limiting the spring and summer seasons, or things that often thrive during the autumn and winter seasons.

Because hydroponic systems also relinquish control of temperature, nutrient levels, humidity, ventilation, and other factors every single day, growers who choose hydroponics do not need their winter or autumn crops to survive only in the season. Is. Go ahead and grow tomatoes in January - due to your hydro system, they can start juicier than ever.

7. Get larger, more reliable,

Harvest while crops can reduce the likelihood of growing crops within the offseason and losing crops from diseases or pests, which may represent your savings in your bottom line, leading to the loss of your harvest. Dimensions and quality improve. Help increase your profit-per-square-foot even more.

Hydroponics often tries to boost crop reliability and quality due to better nutrient and water delivery to growers. When everything has direct use up to each plant's root, it should grow and flower; your greenhouse is a great way to refer to a more significant and better crop than you are ready to receive within the soil.

8. Automatic and leftover

One of the main drains on any producer's budget, the substantial labor cost needed to bring a seedbed from seed to harvest or to germinate. This task can include everything from fighting weeds and fighting pests to easily monitoring and adjusting environmental controls to keep things optimal. By automating your hydroponic system, you can significantly reduce the amount of labor required to realize an equal - or perhaps better - result.

In a hydroponic system, everything from growth temperature to humidity levels and light levels, nutrient levels, and quality are often automated for ideal delivery, even once you are miles away from your greenhouse. Occur. This is because the automated system can continuously monitor your growing location for changes in conditions and automatically make improvements, saving you the time and energy needed to see and respond to your growing space problems.

CHAPTER 10: PESTS AND DISEASES

According to greenhouse crop professionals, you should know when your crops are sick. From mildew and rust to viruses and root rot, the disease can wreak havoc on your plants. The signs of common diseases must be known to work correctly against the circumstances.

Plant experts also suggest that you become aware only of the types of insects interested in specific plant species. To prevent disease, it is recommended that you only do in-depth research on harmful pests that will be naturally prepared for your crops. The most common greenhouse pests include:

Aphids (plant lice) - small, dull worm clusters in colonies and a tendency to multiply rapidly. Curved stems and leaves are familiar when they are present.

Fungus Gnats - While adults are often found on foliage, the larvae burrow within the soil and prey on root hairs, causing the plant to wilt or grow less vigorously. When fully developed, these gnats have short bodies with long legs and pronounced wings. Noise flies are almost like fungal animals but have fewer antennae, red eyes, darker bodies, and smoky wings. They will be seen resting on any surface within the greenhouse and spread soil pathogens within the greenhouse.

Bloodworms - These insects have bodies and long legs, provoking a recognizable red color. They are often standing water or areas with excessive moisture and can be prey to any algae or organic matter.

Thrips - These small insects have four wings and a row of long hair. They are usually found on the surface of the plant's leaves and that prey on any exile. They tend to attack Kaila, Cyclamen, Cucumber, Fuchsia, Ivy, and Rose plants.

Whiteflies - A more dangerous insect, whiteflies are often immune to pesticides and require close monitoring to eradicate the greenhouse. They need a white, powdery body and are most frequently seen under the leaves of fuchsia, peseta, cucumber, lettuce, and tomato plants.

Leaf miners - These pests begin to damage plants in the form of larvae, feeding between the leaves' outer surfaces. The leaves will lighten and narrow in color as the infection grows and the larvae grow.

Once adults, larvae become flies that lay eggs in pits on leaf surfaces. Unfortunately, most growth stages occur within the leaves; insecticides are not useful in killing or removing leaves. Hand removal and disposal of infected leaves are recommended.

Mealybugs - Small and soft-bodied mealybugs prey on the plant's bark and produce honey, which creates mold on the leaves and stems. They often appear to attack croton plants, hoys, and bamboo palms.

Two-spotted Spider Mites - These pests have two black dots on their abdomen, making them easy to spot. They prey on sap on the leaves' underside, giving the shape of a spotted, yellow, or dried leaf. If an infection is severe, the plants may also be covered during a fine webbing produced by the mite. They are attracted to marigolds, croton, chrysanthemum, roses, impatiens, parlor palms, bamboo palms, and ivy.

Cyclamen mites - Small and semi-transparent, these mites can attack whole plants or simply plant buds. They will be found on African violets, cyclamen, dahlia, and gloxinia. When an infection occurs, the leaves of the plant become discolored or curl.

Slugs and snails - These pests are interested in high humidity climates and often leave stems, flowers, and roots. Holes in the leaves are usually seen with an infection.

Greenhouse Sanitation

Many experienced greenhouse growers have found that maintaining a clean greenhouse will allow you to pay more attention to your crops during the season. To ensure that there is a smooth and productive season, it is recommended that producers should:

- Power wash floors, walls, appliances, and other surfaces.

- Clean floors, walls, and irrigation equipment to prevent future greenhouse disease and infection.

- You only plan on reusing in bleach.

Remove weeds
- Inspect curtains and coverings for signs of wear and tear and aging.
- Disposal of waste and old pesticides.
- Check the equipment to make sure everything is running correctly.
- The use of biological control agents (BIOCONTROL)
- Natural and beneficial organisms, known as biological control agents, are often introduced to remove their greenhouses and prevent infection. According to a report by the NC State University Department of Entomology, the effectiveness of organisms may depend on several factors: climate, reproduction rate, insect life cycle, and therefore the number of pests involved. Thanks to large scale things, additional research should be done for targeted problems.

Biocontrol agents naturally help control infection, but agents take time to spread and hunt prey. Thanks to the delay, it is recommended that agents be left at the primary signal of pests during the greenhouse. If your conservatory is already heavy, experts recommend using pesticide soap or non-residual pesticides on crops to return the number of problems before discharge with bio-pesticide agents. However, it is essential to note that pesticide treatment should be limited. Crop experts warn that if too many treatments are used, biological control agents may not be effective.

Treaty changes

Many pests and diseases are critical to the success of hot and thrive in humid environments, so the temperature and humidity of the greenhouse. Experts suggest that there is a method of regulating temperature and humidity using natural ventilation. These systems allow fresh air to be sieved to aid greenhouse width, temperature and humidity control, air circulation, and CO_2 / oxygen replacement.

Open-air air can benefit plants through evaporation and strengthening of cell membranes, helping them to stay healthy. Meanwhile, continuous air movement creates a similar situation throughout the greenhouse. With similar conditions, greenhouse hot spots are eliminated, and high humidity percentages are reduced and controlled, eliminating the breeding grounds for pests and disease.

Monitoring and Recording
A Michigan State University Agio Research Report states that crop monitoring is essential when maintaining a successful greenhouse. It is recommended that each producer prepare an idea or schedule so that specific sections or rows of their greenhouses can be closely examined every day. To explore the plants, you should bend the leaves and check for discoloration. The report also urges growers to remove plants from their pots and inspect the roots for signs of root pathogens. Inspection time, you should get in the search:

It is suggested that you simply trap yellow, blue, or white sticky plant level. Look for activity and identify heavily affected areas—distinctive colors aid in the attraction of some insects. Yellow nets attract thrips, whiteflies, fungus gannets, and winged aphids, while blue traps primarily attract thrips. A white mesh can help identify fungal glands as full-grown adults. Greenhouse Management magazine recommends using one to 2 cards per 500 to 1,000 square feet. Cards must be replaced weekly.

Greenhouse Canada proposes the use of long sticky tapes to pull and hold insects for managing pests on a large scale. They are going to help reduce infection, giving you more control over your greenhouse environment.

When treating your greenhouse for disease and pests, it is advisable to place indicators in places where an infection occurs. If you spray a plant with growth regulators, pesticides, or fungicides, you will use colored belts to indicate this.

Automation to prevent GREENHOUSE INFESTATION and DISEASE

is a modern version of traditional, manual greenhouses; automated greenhouses enhance climate control to support and protect crops? With the implementation of motors, sensors, and interface boxes, many daily greenhouse maintenance tasks can occur automatically without producers' help.

Automatic climate controllers electronically control greenhouse components such as vent motors and individual movements. Once detected with specified programming, climate controllers ensure uniform temperature and humidity, helping to prevent the breeding of pests and diseases.

However, climate control is not the only benefit of greenhouse automation. Our automated ventilation systems use:

SUPERIOR RELIABILITY

With our lightweight, high torque, low voltage motors, curtain systems operate with fewer moving parts and space requirements than comparable systems. This ensures fewer mechanical issues over time.

EFFORTLESS internal control

ventilation systems, fans, and heaters are often connected to and controlled by one easy-to-use unit. In combination with programming, timers and sensors activate components to take care of specified greenhouse conditions, helping producers' efficiency.

Increased energy

Thanks to solar controllers that facilitate, greenhouses are often automated with energy provided by the sun. This not only helps in reducing energy costs but also provides an additional option and facility to grow in greenhouses in remote solar locations.

Overall, greenhouses with automation are beneficial in some ways, including managing and preventing plant pests and disease. If you are trying to figure out how to increase labor back, save on energy costs, and improve your crops' health, automation may also be the answer you are expecting.

CHAPTER 11: TEMPERATURE AND LIGHT REQUIREMENTS OF YOUR PLANT

One important thing about maintaining plants is that lighting. The speed of your growth and length of time a plant is active depends on the amount of sunlight it receives. Light energy is employed in photosynthesis, the most primary metabolism of the plant. There are three areas to consider when determining sunlight's effect on plant growth: intensity, duration, and quality.

Light intensity

Light intensity affects fertilizer, stem length, leaf color, and flower formation. Generally, plants grown in low light tend to have delicate green leaves. A similar plant grown in very bright light has small, superior branches and large, dark green leaves.

Light exposure

Plants are often classified to suit their lighting requirements, such as high, medium, and low light conditions. The intensity of sunlight from the inside plant depends on the proximity of the sun source to the plant. The power of the candle decreases rapidly as the distance from the incense source increases. The window's direction during a house or office affects the intensity of natural sunlight the plants receive. The most important of the southern exposures is intense light. Eastern and western exposures receive about 60 percent of southern exposures, while northern exposures receive 20 percent of the intensity of southern exposures. Southern exposure is the warmest, eastern, and western coldest, and a northern exposure is the best. Other factors such as curtains, trees outside the window, weather, weather of the year, shade from other buildings, and window cleaning also affect the candle's power. Reflective, light-colored surfaces extend candlepower inside a home or office, while dark surfaces have less candlepower.

Directional Exposure:

Day and Night:

The length or duration of sunlight received by plants has some significance also. Poinsettias, kalanchoes, and yuletide cactus flower for only 11 hours or less (short-day plants). Some plants only bloom when the day is over 11 hours (long-growing plants), while others are not sensitive to day length in the least (day-neutral plants).

Day length:

Plants are exposed to light by increasing time (duration), often impervious to catching less candlepower, as the plant's flowering cycle is not sensitive to day length. The increased light duration allows the plant to make enough food to survive and grow. However, plants require some darkness to grow correctly and are exposed to light for up to 16 hours per day. Excessive sunlight is harmful as insufficient. When a plant receives an excessive amount of direct light, the leaves turn yellow, sometimes burn, turn brown and die. Therefore, protect plants from excessive sunlight during the summer months.

Complimentary Lighting:

Additional lighting is often equipped with either incandescent or fluorescent lights. Incandescent lights produce an excellent deal of heat and do not use electricity very efficiently. If there is artificial light that is the only sunlight source for growing plants, the standard of sunlight or wavelength should be considered. Plants require mostly blue and red light for photosynthesis; except for the flower, infrared is required. Incandescent light produces red primarily and some infrared, but little or no blue light. Fluorescent light corresponds to the amount of phosphorus employed by the manufacturer. Quiet-white light makes blue principally light and low in red light; They are calm enough to quietly position on the verge of plants. Leafy plants grow well under a cool-white, fluorescent light, while blooming plants require additional infrared. It will be supplied by incandescent lights or unique gardening fluorescent lights.

Temperature

Most plants tolerate normal temperature fluctuations. Generally, leaf plants grow best between 70 ° and 80 ° F during the day and between 60 ° and 68 ° F at night. Most flowering plants prefer a similar daytime temperature range but grow best when nighttime temperatures rise from 55 ° to 60 ° F.
Low nighttime temperature helps the plant: loss of moisture intensifies the flower's color and prolongs the height's life. Extremely low or high temperatures can cause plant stress, inhibiting growth or an unclear appearance and promoting foliage damage or drop. Quiet night temperatures are more desirable for plant growth than high temperatures. A simple rule of thumb is to keep the night temperature 10 to fifteen degrees below the day temperature.

Atmospheric humidity is expressed as the percentage of moisture in the air. This is important for plants in modulating moisture loss and temperature. There are many ways to increase the proportions around plants. A humidifier is often associated with heating or ventilation within a home or office. Also, gravel trays with a constant moisture level are usually placed under pots or containers. The moisture evaporates around pebbles, the ratio increases in the area around the plants.

Conclusion

As the days get shorter with winter approaches and you find yourself inside more often, spending time reviewing greenhouse or hoop house production opportunities. If you choose to travel for it, then the time has come to figure out your production plan and shopping and sowing dates. Wherever you live, you will grow a greenhouse full of crops, ready for the market through winter and the earliest spring!

www.ingramcontent.com/pod-product-compliance
Lightning Source LLC
Chambersburg PA
CBHW070101120526
44589CB00033B/1199